Special Education:

Best Practices in Focus

BY

Michael J. Cohen, M.S. Ed

Triangulum Academic Publishing, 2015

[This page left intentionally blank]

Special Education: Best Practices in Focus

First Edition 2015

ISBN: 978-0692489819

Published via Triangulum Academic Publishing; printed by CreateSpace

PRINTED IN THE UNITED STATES OF AMERICA

[This page left intentionally blank]

Table of Contents

Preface

The objective of this book is to provide educators a comprehensive yet concise collection of best practices for special education. Albeit there is seemingly no end to the amount of information available, it can seem a daunting task to finding material distilled and ready for practical application. In this work, the reader will find sixteen short chapters detailing some of the most essential methodologies to employ in the classroom. In an effort to create a book applicable to both the special education and general education teacher, some of the most essential learning theories are discussed. It is my hope that you find this book beneficial and informative in your teaching.

Best wishes for your continued success in education,

Michael J. Cohen, M.S.Ed

[This page left intentionally blank]

About the author

Michael J. Cohen, M.S.Ed

Michael Cohen received his Masters in Education from Northcentral University and was initiated into the educational honor societies of Pi Lambda Theta and Kappa Delta Pi. The author, also known as Yosef M. Cohen in Hebrew, received rabbinical ordination in 2011. He is currently a professor of Talmud in a tertiary level yeshiva in Passaic, New Jersey where he lives with his wife and three children. This is his first publication.

Chapter 1: Accommodations and Modifications in Special Education

An important aspect of special education involves appropriate accommodations and modifications of curricula for the exceptional student. This chapter highlights the difference between accommodations and modifications. In addition, the role accommodations play in self-sufficiency is explored. Furthermore, the prevalence of accommodations employed is discussed.

Definition of Accommodations and Modifications

Educational accommodations are defined as alterations in the method of delivery of the curricula without changing the actual material being studied. In contrast, educational modifications are changes made in the actual curricula in order to assist the learning process of students with disabilities (Hallahan, Kauffman & Pullen, 2009, p. 64). For example, a student with low vision who is supplied with large print text books or auditory means of study would be considered an accommodation; whereas allowing a student to skip sections of required reading or a section of a test would be a modification.

According to the Individuals with Disabilities Education Act of 2004 (IDEA 2004), modifications resulting in an alternate curriculum are only appropriate for the small percentage of exceptional students that cannot partake of the general curriculum due to the severity of their disabilities (Raymond, 2012, p. 67). Instead, alternate curricula created for students with severe and profound intellectual disabilities focus on life skills and vocational skills (Hallahan, et al., 2009, p. 168).

Prevalence of Accommodations

Currently, nearly two-thirds of exceptional students receive accommodations on high stakes statewide assessment tests. The most common accommodations are alternate test settings, extension of time and read-aloud accommodations (Luke & Schwartz, 2007, p.6; Hallahan, Kauffman & Pullen, 2009, p. 213). Hallahan et al. note (p. 167) one variation of time extension is the presentation of smaller sections of the test over the course of several days. Some exceptional students find tests more manageable if presented piecemeal for them to concentrate on one segment at a time. Nevertheless, Luke and Schwartz acknowledge the concern that some teachers are overusing accommodations by simply applying whatever they think might augment a student's score (p. 8). Instead, best practices dictate the proper alignment of specific accommodations for the individual student (Taylor, 2009, pp. 20-22). In particular, extension of time is not beneficial for students that lack proper time management skills; and read-aloud accommodations can increase the difficulty of some types of test questions. Moreover, Taylor cautions that both extended time and read-aloud accommodations pose a danger of inflated test scores when not properly administered. In contrast, little, if any, evidence exists for not using alternate testing settings. In reality, for students who are accustomed to small group accommodations such as a resource room, small group testing may be the most natural test setting for these students (Taylor, 2009, p. 21).

Accommodations and Student Learning

Luke and Schwartz (2007, p. 5) posit that as long as students without disabilities would not be able to boost their scores when given the same accommodation, the application of an accommodation would not be considered an unfair advantage for the exceptional student. Still, many researchers note that scores obtained via accommodations cannot always be equally compared to scores of general education students obtained in a non-accommodated setting (p. 7). In particular, Hallahan, Kauffman and Pullen (2009, pp. 213-214) consider accommodations that are not custom tailored to the specific needs of an individual student as an unfair advantage and not indicative of the students mastery, or lack of, material being tested. This would indicate that when used correctly, accommodations can be viewed as positive tools for student learning. Additionally, accommodations can be viewed as playing an important role in the goal of self-sufficiency and self-determination for the exceptional student population. Hallahan et al. (2009, p. 216) report that exceptional students who display perseverance in their studies and long term participation in special educational assistance are more likely to succeed in their goals of self-determination. The proper use of educational accommodations throughout the school years can bolster the positive feeling of self-sufficiency by allowing the student to display his or her academic grasp of the subject matter without the hindrance of learning disabilities distorting test scores.

Chapter 2: EBD in Focus: ADHD

Currently, one of the most prevalent Emotional and Behavioral disorders (EBD) is Attention Deficit and Hyperactivity Disorder (ADHD) (Geng, 2011; Webber & Plotts, 2008). This chapter will highlight the various challenges of ADHD in the classroom setting. The definition, origin, prevalence and best practices for intervention will be advanced. Additionally, interventions suitable for an inclusive classroom scenario will be emphasized.

Definition and Prevalence in Children

Before discussing prevalence of ADHD, it would be prudent to preface the discussion with reviewing definition of ADHD. ADHD is considered a neurobiological developmental disability (Webber & Plotts, 2008). In particular, individuals with ADHD typically exhibit persistent inattention and distractibility with frequent and intense impulsivity (Geng, 2011). For a student with ADHD, the aforementioned characteristics create difficulties in his or her learning during classroom activities.

Although estimates vary, Webber and Plotts (2008) note that ADHD prevalence is on the rise with approximately five percent of students diagnosed as ADHD. However, research on ADHD prevalence can range between three to twenty percent. Several rationales to clarify the large divergence of prevalence will be presented. According to Webber and Plotts (2008), this divergence can be explained on the criteria employed during research. Statistical data presented in research may be based on clinical settings or on community settings such as parental or teacher recognition of ADHD. In contrast, Imeraj, et. al.(2013) posit a distinct approach to ADHD prevalence discrepancy. According to Imeraj et. al.(2013), ADHD prevalence can vary based on teacher presence and teaching ability in the classroom. Neophyte educators may report ADHD in the classroom more often due to lack of experience in management of students with ADHD symptoms. Additionally, variations can result based on observations between small and large group settings, with higher manifestations of ADHD in larger group scenarios (Imeraj, et. al., 2013). Imeraj et. al. (2013) offer another possibility to explain the discrepancies reported for ADHD prevalence can be based on the duration of time in observing students. For example, observations for one academic period or other short time span may report less ADHD than observation for a whole day's duration. Moreover, ADHD more often affects males than females with a ratio of one female per six males in clinical studies (Webber & Plotts, 2008).

ADHD in the Classroom

Students with ADHD can pose several educational challenges in the classroom (Webber & Plotts, 2008). Firstly, curricula and teaching methods may need to be modified to facilitate learning. Moreover, the teacher must create a balance between educational needs of the individual with ADHD and yet not take away from the learning process of the general student population in the classroom (Imeraj, et. al., 2013). Webber and Plotts (2008) note the importance for educators to familiarize themselves with ADHD characteristics and proper teaching strategies and best practices to employ in the classroom. Likewise, Geng (2011) considers knowledge of ADHD among classroom educators a necessary matter in order to share common parlance and effective communication with other professionals and special education teachers who share responsibility for contributing to the educational and overall wellbeing of students with ADHD.

ADHD Best Practices in the Classroom

A variety of methodologies for the inclusive classroom exist to facilitate instruction of the ADHD student population. Geng (2011) considers best practices to combine verbal and non-verbal strategies to engage and focus the attention of students with ADHD on lesson and curriculum activities. Verbal strategies can include repeated instructions, using the student's name to draw attention and shorter or concise directives. Likewise, non-verbal strategies that can be used separately or in connection to verbal strategies can include visual cues such as supplementary information on the board or use of additional colored markers to present data in a more exciting fashion.

Imeraj, et. al., (2013) researched the ability for students with ADHD to stay on task in a variety of classroom settings to determine which method of instruction would be most beneficial. The conclusion of the above mentioned researchers indicates that small group activities provided the most structure for students with ADHD to engage in focused learning. Imeraj et. al. (2013) consider high level of organization coupled with the student's active role and collaboration with peers to be prominent aspects of the success of small group activities for the ADHD population. In contrast, Imeraj et. al. (2013) note that individual assignments provided significantly less stimulus for focusing and resulted in higher off-task behaviors. Moreover, the correlation between focused attention and the subject matter was established. Science, mathematics and language studies produced a greater amount of off-task behavior in comparison to music and art disciplines (Imerjai, et. al., 2013). Consequently, Imeraj et. al. (2013) regards supervision of transition from one academic activity or subject to another to likewise be considered among best practices to sustain the focus and attention of students with ADHD during the transition.

To further pique interest and focus in classroom activities, Webber and Plotts (2008) suggest several best practices to this end. It is vital to prepare curricula in a clear fashion with an organized structure. This will facilitate focus. Moreover, educators must be cognizant of academic abilities of students with ADHD and adjust curricula accordingly. In addition, best practices dictate focus on maintaining a flow of instruction without disruption. Accordingly, trivial disturbance generated by students with ADHD should be ignored.

Best practices employed in the classroom must be supplemented by similar support and strategies at home to provide and maintain advancement made in the classroom (Pfiffner, Villodas, Kaiser, Rooney, & McBurnett, 2013). Thus, Pfiffner et. al. consider it vital that teachers be aware of this concept and work together with parents of ADHD students to ensure supportive ADHD methodologies are being enforced at home. In particular, teachers can play a vital role in educating parent training during parent-teacher conferences and other meetings. In turn, parents knowledgeable concerning ADHD learning methods will be better equipped to help with homework and bolster organizational skills.

Chapter 3: Learning Styles of Students with Mild Learning Disabilities

Knowledge of the learning styles and characteristics of the learning disabled population is crucial for educators to best employ useful and direct teaching methods. This chapter will focus on the various learning styles and motivational factors typical of students with mild learning disabilities and best practices for educators to foster educational success.

Learning Characteristics

In general, students with mild learning disabilities are able to advance through various stages of learning albeit at a slower pace. Educators must be mindful and considerate of this by allowing extra time and materials or other educational accommodations if needed (Raymond, 2012, p. 259). Educational accommodations are defined as modifications in the method of delivery of the curricula without changing the actual material being studied (Hallahan, Kauffman & Pullen, 2009, p. 64).

Behavioral Patterns

Behavioral patterns and social interactions play an important role in the academic learning ability of students with mild learning disabilities (Raymond, 2012, p. 259). Academically speaking, research indicates that students with mild learning disabilities often report feeling greater social restraint and rejection with their classroom peers (Vauhgin, Elbaum, Schumm & Huges, 1998, p. 429). To compensate, some students with learning difficulties act out inappropriately in the classroom for attention. Although it is necessary to appropriately reprimand classroom disturbance, teachers must be cognizant of the underlying causes. Often, students with learning disabilities feel frustrated at their inability to perform at the pace of their peers and lack of ability to keep up to classroom activities (Hallahan, Kauffman & Pullen, 2009, p. 163). Best practices dictate that teachers provide positive motivation for students with mild learning disabilities, which in turn, will lead to an increased sense of accomplishment and decrease in behavioral interruptions in the classroom (Raymond, 2012, pp. 265-266).

Motivational Factors

It is judicious that educators be cognizant with the theory and various forms of academic motivation since students with mild disabilities often present substantial motivation concerns in the classroom (Hallahan, Kauffman & Pullen, 2009, p. 163). Raymond (2012, pp. 261-262) considers motivational factors to be divided into two categories based on the source of the motivation. Intrinsic motivation is the natural desire to learn the subject matter. Generally, a learner will have natural motivation when he or she feels confident in their ability to achieve and that the curricula are intellectually appealing. In addition, success further fosters intrinsic motivational self-confidence.

Extrinsic motivation is presented to the student by an outside source, usually the teacher or parents in the form of rewards for performing well, or conversely punishment for negative actions or the lack of performing the desired behavior. Educators must be mindful that although creating a short-time or temporary incentive program may be warranted, prolonged use of a rewards program rarely translates into intrinsic motivation and actual less interest in the subject.

Best practices for fostering motivation in the learning disabled population include feedback on work that helps students make and realize the correlations between their mistakes and the correct answers. This will promote motivational skills to a fuller understanding of the correlation of the original question or assignment and the correct response (Berkely, Mastropieri, Scruggs, 2011, p. 19).

Additionally, Raymond (2012, p. 262) posits that explaining how incorrect answers were wrong in a positive fashion further empowers feelings of self-determination that plays a direct role in motivation with the ultimate goal of stimulating intrinsic motivational feelings. Understanding the learning characteristics of students with mild disabilities vis-à-vis self-determination is an important aspect of academic performance (and general life skills) that teachers must foster in the classroom (p. 272). Berkely, Mastropieri and Scruggs (2011, pp. 19-20) note this is especially important for students with reading difficulties because proper motivation and determination is necessary for critical reading that requires higher thinking and cognitive skills necessary for reading comprehension. In particular, best practices for students with reading disabilities include Reading Comprehension Strategies (RCD). RCD is composed of several skills that aim to increase the student's comprehension of the reading material and the ability to extrapolate necessary information. First, the student must learn to realize the "purpose" of the reading. What is the reader's aim and intention of reading the selected material? Next, students are to instructed to remember to actively read using all their available background knowledge to place the reading material in context. The teacher then encourages the student to self-question him or herself regarding the selected reading. Are there any apparent contradictions? What can I infer from what I just read? Finally, summarization skills are presented to foster a clear end-result gestalt of the reading material so the student can mentally refer to concrete concepts when answering questions on the reading.

Chapter 4: Models of EBD Treatment

Regarding Emotional and Behavioral Disabilities (EBD), there is no theoretical model monolith to explain the cause and provide a methodology of intervention. It is prudent for educators to be knowledgeable in the variety EBD model in order to gain the necessary parlance in communicating with other special education professionals that subscribe to a different model then oneself (Webber & Plotts, 2008). Therefore, this chapter will discuss and explore the various models used to understand EBD.

The Source of EBD

Regardless of the model presented to remediate EBD, it is prudent to be knowledgeable as to what causes EBD. Unfortunately, although the source of EBD is currently unknown, there are four main factors that are considered causes. An actual case of EBD is most often a composite of two or more factors (in varying degrees). Research records that six to ten percent of children display persistent EBD behavior and having two of more conditions, known as comorbidity, is not uncommon (Webber & Plotts, 2008).Each of the five theoretical models of EBD emphasize one or more factors over the others. One aspect is the biological imbalance of a genetic or biochemical nature. Another factor is family dynamics that may trigger social disorders should there be discord or dysfunction in the household. Likewise, school factors such as negative social interactions at school may contribute to disorders. Cultural considerations can also foster behavioral issues via inappropriate exposure to violence and negative influence (Raymond, 2012).

The Biophysical Model

The biophysical model posits that biological factors, such a hormonal, chemical or neurological imbalances cause EBD. Webber and Plotts (2008) note that some researchers surmise that such imbalances are ultimately the result of genetic mutations. Currently, however, there is not enough research in this approach to substantiate this position conclusively. Nevertheless, research in epigenetics suggests a relationship between an individual's genetic makeup and the impact of his or her environment on how particular genes are triggered ("Psychology: Epigenetics", 2013). This aspect of epigenetics plays a role in the classic discussion as what role nature versus nurture has on an individual's behavior and temperament. Even in scenarios where biological factors can be attributed as the origin of the individual's EBD, biological factors are hardly ever the exclusive cause of EBD. Rather, environmental interactions can set off underlying biological triggers (Raymond, 2012).

When biological factors are considered the main attribution for EBD, current best practices employ the use of drug therapy through medications to create hormonal or chemical homeostasis. The prevalence for drug therapy is high, with slightly over half of all EBD elementary students on some form of drug therapy (Webber & Plotts, 2008). The type of medication prescribed is based on the variety of EBD expressed. For example, Ritalin is often the drug of choice in children with Attention Deficit (AD) and or Attention Deficit Hyperactivity Disorder (ADHD). As with any drug usage, it is prudent that parents and educators be cognizant of known side-effects and report and occurrences to medical personnel responsible for prescription (Webber & Plotts, 2008).

The Psychodynamic Model

The psychodynamic model is based on the theory that EBD is due to dysfunctional psychological processes and proper treatment involves the fostering and facilitation normative emotional development (Webber & Plotts, 2008).

According to the psychodynamic model, treatment is based on providing the student with a supportive educational atmosphere and creating positive learning experiences (Raymond, 2012). Moreover, the earlier such interventions are employed, the better are the chances that the treatment will be successful (Thomas & Kevin, 2010). In addition to early intervention, it is vital that the educator be sensitive and in-tune with characteristics associated with the EBD population including perceptions and feelings and be able and available to listen carefully to the student (Wood, 1995).

In the psychodynamic model, various therapeutic designs to provide intervention and remediation are advanced. Webber and Plotts (2008) consider the reality therapy and group process among current best practices. The reality therapy advances the notion that emphasis teaching responsibility, reality and right-and-wrong. Instruction of these three points, commonly referred to as the "three R's", provide a certain amount of structure, organization and order necessary for academic learning in school.

In particular, responsibility is the major theme of the model. As behavioral disruption is a common issue with EBD students, responsibility inculcates the ability to learn in a classroom setting without infringing on the educational rights of the rest of the student body to learn in a undisturbed manner. This responsibility is further imparted to the student with a coming to terms with reality and the requirements necessary to partake of realistic scenarios. This is especially important as denial or misunderstanding of reality is a common feature of the EBD population. The Right-and-wrong aspect further delineates expected behavior by introducing accepted value judgments and social parlance.

In contrast to reality therapy, group process focuses on solving problems, personal crises and behavioral issues in a group setting. In general, the group will contain a teacher along with a school psychologist or other special education personnel to moderate and introduce discussion with a small group of students. This model posits that emphasis on communication skills can best be achieved in a group environment. That said, this model is not recommended in a scenario when the individual requires customized remediation. The group environment can facilitate discussion of common EBD issues such as anger management, bullying, social skills and coping with emotions that can create a sense of camaraderie amongst the student participants and bolster their self-esteem (Webber & Plotts, 2008).

The Cognitive Model

The cognitive model advocates that EBD behaviors are due to flawed understanding of reality and expectations. This theory is equally valid for all human cognition. Namely, the way a person views events and happenings has a direct and strong influence on the individual's behavior. Essentially, via changing the individuals thought process and cognitional perception, he or she will prevail over EBD, or at the very least temper it that it will not interfere (Webber & Plotts, 2008). In addition, the cognitive model aims to empower EBD students with the necessary skills to self-regulate their behavior. This is accomplished in a framework in which cognitive self-regulation of interpersonal dealings and self-control is addressed as Self-Instruction Training (SIT) (Robinson, 2007). To illustrate, Robinson (2007) contends that an EBD student with impulsivity issues can be given verbal reinforcements to discipline the lack of controlling impulses. Slowly, the verbal reinforcements are increased in terms of directly corresponding to the target behavior in a manner that slowly changes the student's cognitive perception of impulse control until the student actually gains mastery or marked improvement in the behavior. This is an excellent example of how the cognitive model can slowly alter the student's cognition to a normative behavior.

This SIT paradigm of impulse control used by Robinson (2007) can be applied to any behavior in need of modification. However, Webber and Plotts (2008) consider it essential and best practices for SIT to proceed in the following five steps. First, the educator verbalizes the target behavior while performing that behavior. Next, the student is instructed to perform the same behavior as the educator verbalizes the instructions. Then the student performs the task again while whispering the instructions. Lastly, the student performs the task with only concealed and secret-like verbalizations.

SIT can further be enhanced through the student's self-monitoring. A chart can be created in which the student records the target behavior. This creates a very real and powerful self-awareness for the student that will facilitate the modification of behavior process. Moreover, it will allow the teacher and student to record the history of growth for review (Webber & Plotts, 2008).

The Ecological Model

The ecological or systems model places a balance of remediation on individual behavior and the interaction of the surrounding environment. This model aims at behavioral modification based on modifying influences from the surrounding environment (Webber & Plotts, 2008). This is especially valuable in scenarios involving school violence or aggressive behavior (Thomas & Kevin, 2010). However, Thomas and Kevin (2010) note the success of minimizing exposure to violent influences is tempered if experiences at home continue to contribute to violence. To illustrate, video games, television shows and movies that feature violence tend to promote and endorse this behavior in children. In such scenarios where negative environmental influences emerge from the home, Webber and Plotts (2008) consider a systems approach among best practices to influence parental decisions regarding such environmental factors. A systems approach can offer family traditional family therapy where positive and healthy family dynamics can be presented to emulate and incorporate into a family. A sampling of healthy family structure include creating and maintaining a rule system with a clear hierarchy of parental authority, continuous nurturing behavior in a steady fashion from the parents, and the ability to be flexible and adjust to family changes or crises.

The Behavioral Model

In comparison to the above mentioned models, the behavioral model is singular for attributing EBD symptoms directly to an individual's personal experiences and environmental surroundings (Webber & Plotts, 2008). Educational advocates of the behavioral model contend that all EBD behaviors in moderation are not considered disabling or problematic. Rather, the frequency and extreme aspect are the cause of concern. Thus, the behavior expressed is not the concern, but rather the inability to moderate it appropriately (Robinson, 2004).

In this model, remediation best practices consist of modeling proper use and regulation of behavior based on social observation of peers (Raymond, 2012). Positive incentives for following correct academic and social norms of fellow students reinforce these behaviors in the student. Reinforcements can be of the immediate nature, such as extra recess, or can be long term using a token economy (Webber & Plotts, 2008). A token economy adds a "token" to the students chart or other means of recording. For example, in younger grades this may be a sticker chart, with the accumulation of stickers as the tokens. This strategy allows for the accrual of behavioral reinforcement with a sense of accountability to finish the chart (Webber & Plotts, 2008; Raymond, 2012).

Chapter 5: Applying the Cognitive Model in the School Setting

This chapter will focus on the best practices advanced by the cognitive model for students with Emotional and Behavioral Disabilities (EBD) discussed in the previous chapter. In particular, emphasis will be on practical application in the school and classroom setting.

The Theory of the Cognitive Model

Before discussing specifics of how best to employ the cognitive model in a school environment, it is prudent to discuss the theory and definition. The cognitive model posits that the manner in which people think, or cognition, directly correlates and impacts an individual's perception of reality and his or her environment. Individuals exhibiting EBD behaviors are due to a flawed understanding of reality and expectations (Webber & Plotts, 2008). Such distortions can include methods and skills for problem solving, appropriate expression of anger, phobias or frustration and effective communication skills (Robinson, Smith & Miller, 2002).

Thus, the Cognitive model aims to reorient the cognitive understanding to facilitate integration with others (Webber & Plotts, 2008). In particular, this is accomplished via introducing conditioning. Conditioning is the pairing of a reinforcer or punisher to a target behavior to strengthen or weaken it. In turn, conditioning facilitates self-regulation of behaviors that will allow the student to participate in activities (Robinson, 2007). Mayer, Lochman and Van Acker (2005) offer several advantages posed by the cognitive model's emphasis on self-regulation. In contrast to other theoretical models that place emphasis on external controls, self-regulations' slow and natural indoctrination of reality is viewed as participating by one's own volition by the student. Models that create an external requirement are more likely to be encountered by resistance. Furthermore, focus on external controls may lead to improvement in behavior only in scenarios similar to the kind worked at and will not lead to a generalized behavior that will produce the same consistent results.

Application of the Cognitive Model at School

Among best practices of the cognitive model to employ a conditioning effect for EBD students is Self-Instructional Training (SIT) (Robinson 2007; Webber & Plotts, 2008). Webber and Plotts (2008) note that practical application of SIT should adhere to the following five steps. Initially, the teacher verbalizes the target behavior while performing that action. The student is then instructed to perform the same activity as the educator verbalizes the instructions. Subsequently, the student performs the task again while whispering the instructions. Finally, the student performs the task with only hinted verbalizations. The SIT procedure is repeated while the verbal reinforcements are increased in terms of directly corresponding to the target behavior in a fashion that slowly changes the student's cognitive perception of self-regulating the behavior (Robinson, 2007).

Furthermore self-instructional practices like SIT can further be enhanced through self-monitoring. Self-monitoring is a process where the EBD student creates a chart or other indicator of progress can be utilized in which the student records the target behavior being achieved. This creates a very real and powerful self-awareness for the student that will facilitate the modification of behavior process. In addition, it will allow the educator and student to record the history of growth for later review (Webber & Plotts, 2008).

Additionally, it is prudent to maintain learned cognitive self-regulation skills by means of supplementary lessons and practices. Robinson, Smith and Miller (2002) contend that repeated booster activities of gained self-regulation skills directly correlate to sustained application of the target behavior. Such activities to reinforce self-regulation is best determined on an individual basis that can range from once a week to bi-monthly based on the educator's discretion.

Difficulties in Application

Practical application of the cognitive model for the EBD student population in school can pose several challenges. A large percentage of EBD students display disruptive and inappropriate behavior in the classroom which make learning difficult for their peers (Webber & Plotts, 2008). Therefore self-regulation practices can be complicated to employ in a group setting such a the general classroom. Educators must be cognizant that cognitive methodologies may work best when working on an individual basis (Robinson, Smith & Miller, 2002).

Mayer, Lochman and Van Acker (2005) note that it is common for teachers to utilize aspects of the cognitive model in their classrooms for EBD students. They raise the inquiry if practical application of segments of cognitive theory model can be employed out of context in the classroom. Mayer et. al. ponder if extracting a selection of techniques may undermine the efficacy of the model, as research has only demonstrated empirical evidence for application of the cognitive model in its entirety. On the other hand, countless educators have had marked success in deciding which practices to utilize. The question remains where is the line of demarcation for educators to decide on their own which practices to choose independent of the corpus of best cognitive practices. Mayer et. al. leave the matter unresolved.

Reflections

After review of the available best practices endorsed by the cognitive model for students with EBD, this writer concurs that self-monitoring via chart or other record keeping is a quiet activity that can be employed in the general classroom without hindrance to the other students. However, perhaps other aspects of self-regulation such as SIT is optimized for pull-out or special education classes. Feasibility of SIT implementation would depend if classroom dynamics can allow such curricula tangents to take place without impeding on the flow of the lesson. Thus, each teacher should use discretion and apply SIT and other self-instructional aspects of cognitive best practices.

Chapter 6: Cognitive Behavior Modification

It is vital for teachers of students with special needs to be ⸴ knowledgeable of the learning styles and characteristics of behavior and thought process associated with exceptional students for educators to best employ useful and direct teaching methods. To this end, cognitive behavior modification (CBM) interventions are considered best practices to create and maintain appropriate classroom behavior and social skills. Several examples of CBM interventions will be discussed and clarified in this chapter.

Origin and Theory of Cognitive Behavior Modification

Essentially, CBM is based on the premise that behavior is arbitrated by cognitive events (such as ones perceptions and thoughts) and alteration or modification in cognition will in turn cause a direct change in behavior (Zirpoli, 2008, p. 339).

Research demonstrates that behavioral intervention, such as CBM, based on cognitive psychology lead to positive and substantial educational gains. In particular, behavioral psychologists posit that the learning process can be viewed in three distinct stages. First, an antecedent for information is provided by an educational stimulant, for example a teacher or textbook, followed by a behavior and consequence of the learner. Thus, this model of learning enables the teacher to focus and direct aspects of the learning process by eliciting desired antecedents and behaviors (Bender, 2008, p. 304).

Cognitive psychologists have further developed and modified the learning model advanced by the behavioral psychologists. They posit that humans have an additional and unique intermediate step linking the antecedent and the behavioral response. This theory of human learning, known as the metacognitive model, emphasizes the human use of Inner Language (Bender, 2008, pp. 326-327). In essence, Inner Language can be defined as thinking about thinking. This involves the active analysis and discrimination of a given antecedent on a conceptual (thing) or symbolic (word) level that will influence the learner's behavior and consequence (Pang, 2010, p. 30). Furthermore, Pang (2010, pp. 30-31) stresses the importance metacognition plays in active learning via self-regulation, academic motivation and critical thinking. This in turn has a direct effect on self-confidence and self-efficacy.

Self-Management Training

Self-management training is an excellent example of CBM best practices. The objective of self-management is to teach the student to conduct his or her behavior properly (Zirpoli, 2008, p. 343). In particular, self-management training methodologies focus on empowering students for behavioral self-efficacy. To this end, self-management training makes use of self-monitoring and self-evaluation as best practices (p. 344). Self-monitoring techniques focus on creating self-awareness of a students' own behavior and bolsters accountability by having the student monitor his or her behavior by recording a target behavior. Often, teachers may keep their own records of behavior to compare to the student to create accountability and accuracy (pp. 344-345). In an effort to encourage student accuracy, a teacher may give an appropriate bonus reward such as extra recess for students that record accurate data (p. 345). In addition to monitoring, it is vital that educators review and evaluate progress and modify the target behavior requirements if needed (p. 346).

Self-Instructional Training

In addition to self-management, self-instructional training is another key CBM intervention method. As previously mentioned, cognition follows a distinct process of perception of surroundings and a chain of mental commands how to interact with the scenario. Self-instructional intervention provides a system of training Self-instructional intervention focuses on providing students with a general statement to employ in a particular classroom scenario (Zirpoli, 2008, p. 353). Over time, this will hopefully refocus the cognitive thought process to become in line with acceptable behavioral thought and action. In order for self-instructional training to be successful, the intervention must be initiated in five specific steps (pp. 353-354). First, the educator must be a model for the student to observe the desired behavior in a target scenario. The teacher verbally relates the self-instructions while performing the task for the student to watch. Next, the student attempts to mimic the observed activity under the educator's guidance. Moreover, the teacher assists the student by saying the self-instructional prompts out loud to facilitate the student's familiarity. The third step, known as overt self-instruction is a transitional phase as the student performs the activity and verbalizes the prompts while the teacher observes and provides necessary feedback. The fourth step, faded self-instruction, furthers the transition to instructional self-efficacy as the student continues to perform the targeted behavior but merely recites the prompts in an undertone. Finally, the student the student attained mastery of the self-instruction and is able to employ the self-instruction independent of any assistance from the teacher.

Problem-Solving Training

Problem-solving training is yet another best practice of CBM interventions (Zirpoli, 2008, p. 359). This intervention method emphasizes making the right social and behavioral decision via formal training. Approaching social conflict in a systematic method can allow students to learn the correct response by adjusting metacognitive perception (pp. 359-360). In particular, formal-solving training identifies the particular target behavior, makes the student cognizant of the issue and clearly delineates what is wrong with the behavior and open discussion of the issue. Furthermore, the teacher and student will discuss appropriate alternatives for that scenario for the future (p. 360). After such dialogue, an intervention plan can be discussed and how best to implement it. By including the student in the step by step process, the student will gain the needed self-confidence and knowledge to pursue the discussed intervention methods (pp. 360-361).

Chapter 7: Anxiety Disorders: Applying Theory in a School Setting

This chapter will focus on the various aspects of anxiety disorders in the school setting. The definition, origin, prevalence and best practices for intervention will be advanced. Additionally, interventions suitable for an inclusive classroom scenario will be emphasized.

Definition and Prevalence in Children

Although anxiety disorders can manifest in several fashions, all share common factors and other facets in this spectrum. Anxiety disorders are characterized as feelings of distress and fear in connection to a specific ordinary activity (Webber & Plotts, 2008). Webber and Plotts (2008) note the most common types of anxiety disorders are separation anxiety, specific phobias and general anxiety. Separation anxiety is extreme worry and nervousness during separation of an attachment figure, such as a parent. Specific phobias are defined by excessive distress in context to a particular scenario. To illustrate, common phobias in children include dogs, heights and dental work. Other examples of anxiety disorder comprise of posttraumatic stress disorder and obsessive-compulsive disorder. In posttraumatic stress disorder a specific repeated traumatic experience produces anxiety, difficulty in concentration and nightmares.

Although estimates vary, a significant amount of research suggests that anxiety disorders affect six to eighteen percent of the general child and adolescent population and is more prevalent in females (Webber & Plotts, 2008; Hallahan, Kaufman & Pullen, 2009). Moreover, it is unclear as to the exact cause of anxiety disorders. Webber and Plotts (2008) consider a variety of factors that can influence anxiety. One approach considers biological and genetic factors. Hallahan et. al. (2009) note that some research indicates a trend of anxiety disorders in families, as children of a parent with an anxiety disorder are more likely to have an anxiety disorder as well. Behavioral and cognitive theories offer a different approach to anxiety disorder influencers. Environmental triggers such as conditioning can lead to learned anxiety. Conditioning can be defined as a specific situation that the individual associates with a fear and adverse reaction which will trigger the same anxiety and fear during the same scenario in the future (Webber & Plotts, 2008). Similarly, incorrect cognitive perceptions of danger can likewise induce anxiety. Webber and Plotts (2208) regard four cognitive inaccuracies that can produce anxiety. Such cognitive mistakes can involve overestimating the severity or likelihood of the target event, or underestimating the ability to cope during the situation or what others can do to help.

Anxiety Disorders in the School Setting

Anxiety can pose social and academic challenges for the student and teacher (Settipani & Kendall, 2012). Settipani and Kendall (2012) consider the administration of tests to determine the severity and specifics of a student's anxiety disorder to better service the student in school as best practices. Such tests include the Anxiety Disorders Interview Schedule for Children (ADIS) and the Child Behavior Checklist (CBLC). In particular, ADIS interviews the parent(s) and child for self-evaluation regarding a variety of common anxiety scenarios to determine severity and triggers of the anxiety. Likewise, the CBLC is an 118 item checklist where a parent chooses a number zero through two with zero representing never, one as sometimes and two as always. Moreover, the CBLC takes into account social outcomes of anxiety disorder. Such questions include popularity of the child, teasing and other aspects of social parlance.

Darhota, Sterling, Hwang and Wood (2013) record that anxiety disorders in children significantly impede daily living skills. This is due to the avoidance of anxiety producing situations which may then be performed by the parent or teacher. For example, the constant evasion of tying one's shoes or buttoning clothing can lead to the lack of basic life skills if parents resign to performing such tasks on behalf of the child. In turn, this can create further complications for older children as parents and teachers assume the child has already mastered basic life skills and proffer less assistance which can reinforce the anxiety.

Classroom Interventions

In the general inclusive classroom, the teacher must employ strategies that will foster academic growth and development in all students (Hallahan, Kaufman & Pullen, 2009). For a student with an anxiety disorder, academic ability is often handicapped by social factors as reluctance to partake in socializing with peers which can undermine learning ability (Darhota, Sterling, Hwang & Wood, 2013; Settipani & Kendall, 2012). Indeed, a direct correlation between social ability vis-à-vis the degree of anxiety has been established as social inability furthers anxiety, which in turn creates a sort of snowball effect (Settipani & Kendall, 2012). Research indicates that the most successful teachers in providing positive emotional support for students have natural skills in advising, relevant experience and background knowledge of the individual student. In general, the teacher's level of education played a minimal role in assessing qualities of successful emotional support (Hallahan, et. al., 2009).

Furthermore, teachers can create time and activities into the curriculum that provide opportunities that promote positive relationship building among classmates. This is especially important for students with anxiety disorders who partake of pull-out or separate services outside the general classroom. By missing part of the general classroom, these students will miss some classroom conversations that may put them at an awkward social position, resulting in staying aloof from further conversation. To compensate, setting aside time in the classroom setting for social interaction can foster conversation in which students with learning disabilities can partake (Raymond, 2012).

Chapter 8: Peer Tutoring

Due to the intricacies of special education, it behooves educators to be cognizant of proper instructional strategies. This chapter focuses on the methodology and benefits of peer tutoring in the inclusive classroom with emphasis on how peers tutoring impacts special education.

Definition of Peer Tutoring

Essentially, peer tutoring is a give-and-take relationship between two students in which one acts as the instructor, or tutor, and the other student learns as a tutee (Olson, Platt & Dieker, 2008, p.269). In the inclusive classroom, general education students can be paired up with students with special needs. A common variation of peer tutoring is when each student takes turns as the tutor for the other student. This variation, known as Reciprocal Peer Tutoring, has additional benefits such as reducing possible resentment for not being solely in the tutee role (Olson, Platt & Dieker, 2008, p.271).

Implementation of Peer Tutoring

When general education students are paired with students with special needs, educators must ascertain if any training is necessary. Just as teachers are trained to educate students with special needs, the success of peer tutoring is dependent on the preparation of the tutor (Stenhoff & Lignugaris, 2007, p. 25). Stenhoff and Lignugaris (2007, p. 27) consider the monitoring of peer tutoring quality to be of utmost importance for the success of the peer tutoring experience. Moreover, peer tutoring is more effective with same-age peers with higher skills in comparison to same-age peers with similar skill level as the tutee. In particular, cross-age peer tutoring demonstrates the weakest academic gain for students with learning disabilities (p. 25).

Additionally, Olson, Platt and Dieker (2008, p.269) regard peer tutoring as a best practice in conjunction with standard teacher directed learning. That is to say, usage of peer tutoring as a complete or nearly complete substitute for teacher directed learning is detrimental for the learning process. Instead, peer tutoring optimally produces best results following teacher directed learning to solidify and practice new knowledge and skills (pp. 299-170).

Emotional Needs of Exceptional Students

In addition to advancing academic goals, peer tutoring plays an important role in fostering social skills (Stenhoff & Lignugaris, 2007, p. 25). Weiner and Tardif (2004, p. 22) report that students with learning disabilities demonstrate that they are cognizant of their academic challenges and often feel inadequate in their academic self-worth. Moreover, students with learning disabilities often feel a greater amount of social rejection in the general classroom in comparison to the general education population (Vauhgin, Elbaum, Schumm & Huges, 1998, p. 429). However, Weiner and Tardif (2004, p. 22) note that their overall nonacademic self-esteem is on par with students without learning disabilities. This information is quite telling regarding the need to implement social building activities into the curricula to bolster interaction amongst students with special needs and the general education student in the inclusive classroom. Consequently, peer tutoring is an excellent choice in the educators repertoire (Olson, Platt & Dieker, 2008, pp.272-273). Particulars of such benefits will be discussed shortly.

Benefits of Peer Tutoring

As mentioned, peer tutoring can pair up general education students with students with special needs such as learning or emotional disabilities to study and grade each other's work. In addition to the academic gain possible from this intervention, peer tutoring can provide a reciprocal social scenario that both students can gain from. Students with social difficulties can learn proper social skills from the general education student, and in turn, the general education student can come to better understand, emphasize and create friendship with a segment of the student population he or she might not have had interactions before. Thus, it is little surprise that Olson, Platt and Dieker (2008, p.270) note that the majority of students have a preference for peer tutoring learning in comparison with teacher-led instruction.

Chapter 9: Emotional Support

An important aspect of intelligence involves emotions. Significant aspects of emotional intelligence includes managing emotions, recognizing emotions in others and handling relationships (Ornstein & Hunkins, 2009, pp.128-129). This essay focuses on the emotional needs of students with learning disabilities. Moreover, among the various roles of the teacher, all educators are expected to support the emotional needs of their students (Phillippo, 2010, p. 2259). Practical strategies for educators in promoting emotional development will be emphasized in this chapter.

Emotional Self-Perception

In order to discuss the appropriate role educators' play in the emotional development of students with learning disabilities, it is prudent to discuss how these students view their own emotional state. Idan and Margalit (2012, p. 3) report that students with learning disabilities demonstrate that they are cognizant of their academic challenges and often feel inadequate in their academic self-worth. Moreover, students with learning disabilities often feel a greater amount of social rejection in the general classroom in comparison to the general education population (Haager & Vaughn, 1995, p. 206; Vauhgin, Elbaum, Schumm & Huges, 1998, p. 429). However, Weiner and Tardif (2004, p. 22) note that their overall nonacademic self-esteem is on par with students without learning disabilities.

Teacher Interactions

The perception of students with learning disabilities have of their general classroom teacher is that the teacher is often more dismissive, less available, and less accommodating towards than then peers without disabilities (Idan & Margalit, 2012, p.3). However, special education teachers were not viewed as such for the same students with learning disabilities. This may be due to a variety of factors such as different academic settings such as smaller classrooms may affect student behavior or the more specific training of special education teachers towards understanding such disabilities (Haager & Vaughn, 1995, p. 206). However, it must be noted that although this is considered the general consensus based on interviews with students with learning disabilities, this should not be misconstrued as an empirical fact, and is based on personal opinion (p.209). Additionally, teachers generally viewed students with learning disabilities as having more behavior problems and below grade level social skills (Weiner & Tardif, 2004, p. 22).

Research indicates that the most successful teachers in providing positive emotional support for students have natural skills in advising, relevant experience and background knowledge of the individual student. In general, the teacher's level of education played a minimal role in assessing qualities of successful emotional support (Phillipo, 2010, p. 2286).

Best Practices for Emotional Support

Raymond (2012, p. 296) notes that there are five elements in providing emotional support for students with learning disabilities that are considered best practices for educators to implement. The first through third principles revolves around the need to support positive social interaction with classmates. Haager and Vaughn (1995, p. 206) consider peer acceptance, or lack of, to be accurate indicator of a student's social difficulty and possible future social problems as well. Raymond (pp. 296-297) recommends that teachers introduce needed social skills to students with learning disabilities prior to group activities that students will need to interact with peers. This will give students the ability to practice social skills in real contexts and allow the teacher to provide feedback to bolster morale if needed and further hone in the student's social skills.

Furthermore, it is prudent for educators to be cognizant and acknowledge that different students have various levels of social comfort in different scenarios. Teachers can create time and activities into the curriculum that provide opportunities that promote positive relationship building amongst classmates. This is especially important for students with learning disabilities who partake of pull-out or separate services outside the general classroom. By missing part of the general classroom, these students will miss some classroom conversations that may put them at an awkward social position, resulting in staying aloof from further conversation. To compensate, setting aside time in the classroom setting for social interaction can foster conversation in which students with learning disabilities can partake of (Raymond, 2012, p. 297).

The fourth and fifth principle which Raymond (p. 296) expounds upon relates to the role the teacher plays in creating and fostering a positive environment of learning for all students. Creating a respectful classroom with a zero tolerance policy towards harassment of any kind is especially conducive for students with learning disabilities to partake in classroom activities. Moreover, a positive and reassuring learning climate can bolster their emotional self-perception by allowing all students to have their needs met and contribute to the classroom activity.

Chapter 10: Disruptive Behavior: Functional Behavioral Assessment

An important aspect of education is the ability to maintain proper classroom decorum. The ability to employ correct assessment protocol is essential for providing behavioral management for individual students and the classroom. The various steps in assessment protocol, implementation via a Functional Behavioral Assessment (FBA) for disruptive classroom behavior will be discussed and clarified in throughout the chapter.

Assessment Protocol

Regardless of the specific behavioral assessment, Zirpoli (2008, pp. 234-235) notes several assessment protocols to consider. In essence, all assessment instruments aim for the ultimate same goal. Namely, identifying the particular cause of the target behavior and how to best intervene to replace with positive and appropriate behavior. The first step, commonly referred to as screening, is to determine whether the disruptive behavior is indeed of a persistent and continuous nature that requires intervention. Once the target behavior is determined to be a persistent issue, it is then necessary to establish which assessment methods will provide the most appropriate means of intervention. Whichever assessment instruments have been chosen, it is vital that educators be skilled in administering and interpreting results (Brookhart, 2011, p. 3). Additionally, it is prudent to explore any possible background reasons for the behavior, such as medical or psychological issues that contribute to the behavior and would need to be factored into the intervention. Educators must then collect data of students behavior in class to determine what classroom dynamics and peer interaction stimulate the target behavior (Zirpoli, 2008, p.235).

In addition to assessment protocol, it is equally essential that educators be proficient in communicating assessment results to parents, students and other teachers (Brookhart, 2011, p. 3). In many scenarios, not one but several educators and other behavioral professionals are involved in development of an intervention plan and effective teamwork and communication is vital (p. 5).

Establishing the Quality of the Assessment

After an assessment plan has been decided upon, it is imperative to establish the veracity of the hypothesis. For example, if the assessment suggests that the behavior occurs during science class in large-group instruction, then if the behavior is not observed in other classes or in a small-group for science activities that would support the assessment theory. On the other hand, should the behavior occur in other activities, or even in a small-group science class, that would demonstrate the assessment to be inaccurate. This would indicate the behavior is not solely related to science, but indicative of larger behavioral issues (Webber & Plotts, 2008, pp. 171-172).

Once the assessment has been deemed to accurate in identifying when the target behavior occurs, the last and most imperative step is the development of an intervention plan. For many students with behavioral disturbance issues, a FBA is employed as an intervention plan. The FBA should focus on prevention and substituting the undesired behavior with replacement behaviors. Prevention focuses on providing an alternate environment that can help alleviate the behavior. For example, if the student has difficulty behaving during a large-group science class, yet does not display the behavior in a small-group setting, then the prevention aspect of the FBA would dictate the move of the student to a small-group setting for science class. The FBA will gradually introduce appropriate replacement behaviors to provide positive responses and behavior from the student (pp. 173-174).

Precision Teaching as Classroom Assessment

After an assessment has been made and a FBA or other modification is ready to employ in the classroom, it is prudent for the educator to confirm and evaluate the quality of the actual assessment. For special education, precision teaching is a practical best practice to affirm the benefits of the assessment in the classroom. Essentially, precision teaching emphasizes checking on the effectiveness and value of any given procedure that the educator deems suitable. Due to the flexibility and adaptability of precision teaching, it is considered a best practice for special education as so many variables can manifest in the classroom (Webber& Plotts, 2008, pp. 174-175).

Furthermore, precision teaching has been shown to be effective for the entire spectrum of learning disabled students ranging from mild to severe in both the elementary and high school settings (p.178). Additionally, the checking and accountability feature serves to not only hold the educator accountable, but creates a liability for the student as well. Webber and Plotts (2008, pp. 217-318) consider including the student in an active role in maintaining and tracking the daily records as an excellent venue for the student to feel empowered to change his or her academic performance.

The flexible nature of precision teaching further promotes the stated goals to change or the form of the negative consequence to alter based on the modified behavior of the student. For example, the teacher might have initially deemed an increase of three to nine math problems for homework as an adequate objective goal for the student. Nevertheless, based on the actual progress of the student, the teacher may amend the goal to be more, less or even zero homework problems. This accommodating feature of precision teaching is extremely receptive to the individual needs of the exceptional student population.

Chapter 11: Metacognitive Interventions

In order for teachers to properly transmit information to students, it is crucial to understand the nature of the learning process. Comprehension of how learning works will allow the educator the ability to employ instructional approaches appropriate for the student body. The study of learning and human behavior is known as cognitive psychology (Bender, 2008, pp. 325-326). Cognitive psychologists aim to understand how humans organize their information, store their knowledge and retrieve that learned information to produce conclusions (Ornstein & Hunkins, 2009, p. 118). Research demonstrates that behavioral intervention based on cognitive psychology lead to positive and substantial educational gains. In particular, behavioral psychologists posit that the learning process can be viewed in three distinct stages. First, an antecedent for information is provided by an educational stimulant, for example a teacher or textbook, followed by a behavior and consequence of the learner. Thus, this model of learning enables the teacher to focus and direct aspects of the learning process by eliciting desired antecedents and behaviors (Bender, 2008, p. 304).

Although there are other methods and theories regarding the process of learning, most teachers, curriculum planners and learning theorists embrace the cognitive oriented approach. One major factor contributing to this trend is that curricula for the classroom are often structured in a problem-solving presentation that reflects the cognitive oriented approach. To illustrate, the bulk of the learning process revolves around the educator talking and students mostly responding, with the textbook as the main source for information to complement the teacher (Ornstein & Hunkins, 2009, pp. 136-137).

Metacognition

Cognitive psychologists have further developed and modified the learning model advanced by the behavioral psychologists. They posit that humans have an additional and unique intermediate step linking the antecedent and the behavioral response. This theory of human learning, known as the metacognitive model, emphasizes the human use of Inner Language (Bender, 2008, pp. 326-327). Essentially, inner language can be defined as thinking about thinking. This involves the active analysis and discrimination of a given antecedent on a conceptual (thing) or symbolic (word) level that will influence the learners' behavior and consequence (Pang, 2010, p. 30). Furthermore, Pang (2010, pp. 30-31) stresses the importance metacognition plays in active learning via self-regulation, academic motivation and critical thinking. This in turn has a direct effect on self-confidence and self-efficacy.

Balance Between the Metacognitive Model and Direct Instruction

Although as mentioned most educators subscribe to the cognitive approach to education, the majority employ a direct instruction method of education where the teacher gives over information and the student plays a more passive role. To further facilitate metacognition, it is prudent that teachers incorporate teaching methods that allow students to take a more active role in the learning process (Ornstein & Hunkins, 2009, p. 137). One such method is the Awareness, Evaluation and Implementation (AEI) model that seeks to create a balance between direct instruction and foster metacognition advancement simultaneously (Pang, 2010, p. 33). AEI aims to procure data from direct instruction and advance that knowledge via metacognition to arrive at a deeper and critical understanding of the curricula. For example, direct instruction may be employed to deliver the information during class, yet the educator can create activities, projects and homework assignments using AEI that require students to critically apply knowledge obtained from direct instruction. Such activities would require answers based on information derived from direct instruction that the student would need to combine with critical thinking for in-depth and higher-thinking derived solutions (pp. 33-34).

Reciprocal Teaching

Although the AEI model is appropriate for all students, learners with learning disabilities may face particular hardship in properly sorting out metacognition skills and their application in the learning process. Consequently, best practices include the use of reciprocal teaching to foster an active role in the learning process amongst students with learning disabilities that can hone their metacognitive functions (Bender, 2008, p. 334). Reciprocal teaching, like AEI, aims to foster metacognitive skills for students to develop higher-thinking and critical analysis. Yet in contrast to AEI, reciprocal teaching does not aim to meld metacognition to direct instruction, but rather to develop the metacognition skills necessary for direct instruction in the first place (Williams, 2010, p. 278). Bender (2008, p. 334) notes that reciprocal teaching allows students to take on the role of the teacher for discussion and to ask questions on a reading passage the other students have read. This trains the student to organize information and strategy planning. Initially, prior to actual implementation of a reciprocal teaching exercise, Williams (2010, pp. 278-279) suggests the teacher to role play the part the student will act by verbally addressing and clarifying the various stages of reciprocal teaching. Essentially, prediction, question generation, summarizing and clarifying are the main components this metacognitive method teaches (Bender, 2008, p. 334; Williams, 2010, p. 278-280). The first skill, prediction, involves the use of clues and indications from the reading material to predict what will ensue. This engages the student to be cognizant of what is being read with information already read to compute a reasonable prediction. Question generation will prompt the student to ask questions that can be inferred from the text. First, the student will be trained to ask and answer questions that have an obvious or clear answer directly from the assigned reading. Subsequently, the student will be prompted to solicit questions that are not explicit in the text, but rather inferred. This can also serve the opening for the student to recognize information that may make up test questions. Next, summarization of the reading material generates ability to merge different points from the text into a unified whole. The student should provide an outline of the major points of the storyline in his or her own words. Finally, clarifying should allow the student to review the reading material and identify any unclear or difficult points. This may be an unknown word, concept or confusion to other ideas expressed in the text. At this point the student should have a deeper gestalt of the reading passage and apply metacognitive skills (Bender, 2008, p. 334; Williams, 2010, p. 278-280). However, for students with learning disabilities, this last step of reciprocal teaching can pose the most difficult part. This is because such students are often unaware that they did not understand a concept in the reading material. Thus, clarification aims to force students to slowly analyze the data by re-checking themselves via clarification (Bender, 2008, p 335).

Chapter 12: Best Practices for Memory Skills: Cognitive Strategies

An important aspect of learning involves the process of proper cognition of concepts and the ability to retain information in long term memory. This chapter focuses on the cognition and memory needs of students with learning disabilities. Moreover, among the various roles of the teacher, all educators are expected to foster and promote development of critical thinking and problem solving skills in which cognitive and memory play a pivotal role. Practical strategies and best practices for educators in promoting cognitive development are emphasized.

Role of Memory in Learning

In order to discuss the appropriate role memory plays in the learning process of students with learning disabilities, it is prudent to discuss the various forms of memory in general. Bender (2008, pp. 82-84) notes that memory is divided into short and long term categories. In particular, short term memory is the ability to retain data for immediate use. Furthermore, the ability to integrate information garnered from short term memory with pre-existing data is referred to as working memory. Additionally, working memory is necessary for almost all academic activities such as following instructions, reading comprehension and mathematical problem solving (Martinussen, & Major, 2011, p. 69). In contrast, long term memory is defined as the ability to retain and access information for an extended period of time.

Students with learning disabilities often display difficulty in practical and efficient use of short term and working memory (Raymond, 2012, p. 203). Additionally, a common problem is the lack of cognitive independence necessary for organizing information for efficient processing. This concern further complicates the learning process of students with learning disabilities by impeding higher critical thinking skills due to the inability to recall relevant data (pp. 203-204). In particular, students with Attention Deficit Hyperactivity Disorder (ADHD) display a considerable handicap in effective use of working memory (Martinussen, & Major, 2011, p. 70).

Definition of Cognitive Strategies

Cognitive strategies focus on fostering independent and self-regulated learners. In particular, cognitive strategies focus on critical thinking skills such as seeking precise and relevant information, exploring options, searching for reasons and viewing the entire situation in its totality (Ornstein & Hunkins, 2009, p.132). Although for most general education students' cognitive skills come naturally, students with learning disabilities often lack these skills. Thus, introduction of these skills and strategies play an important role in the special education curricula (Raymond, 2012, p. 65).

Best Practices for Memory Skills

A wide range of methodologies for memory and cognitive development exist that can be applied in the classroom setting. Best practices can further be divided into instructional considerations and self-regulated skills necessary for higher-thinking. Bender (2008, p. 83) considers creating a classroom environment of minimal distractions coupled with verbal and visual cues of utmost importance. This can be accomplished through verbally bullet-marking the lesson by stating the quantity of examples or the number of points during the lesson. This will cue students to note and organize the various segments of the curricula. Moreover, this can further be enhanced visually via using different colored markers to code different points of the discussion on the board. However, educators must be prudent not to use different colors excessively, as this may create distraction and confusion. Additionally, best practices dictate the use of emphasizing the connection between new material and existing information. This methodology, known as paired associates, is crucial for learners with learning disabilities to alleviate the feeling of random data and properly integrate new and old data together (Raymond, 2012, p. 218).

Bender (2008, p. 86) notes that students with learning disabilities often rely on a simple form of memorization known as rehearsal in which information is repeated over and over. Albeit this drilling is useful for the immediate short term memory needs, it fails to take into account the higher-level cognitive needs of learning and analyzing new data. Instead, it is prudent that educators introduce new information in an organized and orderly fashion to further ease to ability to not only memorize, but foster paired association as well. Raymond (2012, p. 217) considers the use of chunking and clustering as best practices to achieve this goal. Chunking refers to the ability to group related items or concepts that associate to one another. Thus, chunking can foster higher cognitive thought as the student develops greater understanding of the larger gestalt of the lesson. The clustering skill further builds upon chunking by systemizing information in categories that relate to other concepts and categories.

Furthermore, teachers must be cognizant of the particular difficulty ADHD students have with working memory when preparing lesson plans (Raymond, 2012, p. 219). Martinussen and Major (2011, pp. 70-71) consider best practices for ADHD working memory development to provide additional time for the working memory load by providing smaller chunks of a data at a time. Although the concept of chunking was previously discussed as an aide for the general learning disabled population, modifying the curricula into especially small chunks is most helpful for the ADHD student. In addition, the ADHD population often benefits from instruction in general organization skills such as how to maintain an organizer, binder and school books in a useful and orderly fashion that will contribute to focusing on classroom content instead of being busy finding the needed materials during class (Martinussen, & Major, 2011, p. 71).

Chapter 13: Reading and Math Strategies

Reading comprehension is a particular difficulty for the majority of learning disabled students (Bender, 2008, p. 180). Research suggests that young children who fail to learn to use phonemes properly have the potential to lead to serious reading comprehension difficulties. In particular, difficulty in decoding the phonemes of words effects the ability to read smoothly and at a comfortable pace (Hallahan, Kauffman & Pullen, 2009, pp. 196-197). To compensate, best practices dictate emphasis on early reading intervention skills that focus on phonemic awareness. Bender (2008, p. 93-94) describes several skills that improve phonemic mastery. Initially, students must be taught to recognize first sound in words and then distinguish the next phoneme. Educators must then teach the ability to manipulate the phoneme and identify the distinction. Thus, phonemes can be added, deleted or substituted with a different phoneme, resulting in a completely new yet similar word. The ability to distinguish the beginning, middle and end sounds are important skills that influence fluid reading. In addition, emphasis should be placed on dividing sounds within words, as well as blending various sounds into words.

Best practices also include visually dependent strategies. To facilitate reading comprehension, the student is instructed to produce a visual image of the reading assignment. Moreover, the imagery must include the necessary details to understand the story. This skill will cause the student to take a proactive role in identifying key elements in reading by creating the necessity to double-check the consistency of the visual image with the reading material (Bender, 2008, pp.197-198).

Approach to Writing Difficulties

Albeit the majority of language arts difficulties lies in the area of reading, it is prudent that educators be cognizant in the various other aspects of language disabilities. Writing can often pose difficulties for the learning disabled population (Bender, 2008, pp. 204-205). Raymond (pp. 239-240) notes that students with mild learning disabilities often have difficulty with the fine motor skills necessary for producing legible and communicative handwriting. Other students may be able to produce legible handwriting but at a severely slowed and reduced pace that negates the effective ability to write and keep up with the rest of the class. In addition, spelling, limited use of vocabulary and less creativity and organization in writing pose additional difficulties for the learning disabled population.

Due to the various ways writing disabilities are displayed, best practices dictate the necessity to evaluate a student's writing to focus on what is the exact difficulty. For example, students with grammatical and spelling mistakes benefit from word processing skills. Introducing word processing tools such as proofreading skills empower a student with mild learning disorders to check his or her work for mistakes (pp. 241-242). Additional writing difficulties such as ineligible handwriting or writing at a severely reduced pace can be accommodated with the introduction of an electronic or digital typewriter device that can allow the student to type legible notes or assignments and remain at the classroom pace at the same time (p. 241).

Bender (2008, p. 205) presents an additional method of self-appraisal for handwriting via a check-list of several considerations for students. The check-list cues students to be mindful of writing mistakes and difficulties mentioned above prior to submitting written assignments. Students that were prepared to use the card benefited in handwriting and writing over a period of time.

Approach to Dialogue Skills

Research indicates that dialogue skills play an important role in the development of reading and other language art skills (Bender, 2008, pp. 196-197). For students with reading difficulties, Hay, Elias, Fielding-Barnsley, Homel, and Freiberg (2007, p. 402) consider early exposure and more practice with interactive dialogue and emphasis on vocabulary development skills to be best practices. Teachers can foster dialogue skills by engaging students in conversation that requires descriptive and complex thoughts that can bolster an increased ability to focus on these concepts in reading. In turn, dialogue skills are beneficial for the student's self-reading skills, especially oral reading which is considered beginning reading skills, which is necessary to master before preceding to higher level reading skills (Raymond, 2012, p. 238). Bender (2008, p. 197) notes an additional benefit dialogue skills is the ability to focus on whole phrases as opposed to each individual word. In dialogue, listeners focus on the complete phrase or sentence, and this skill, over time, can be transferred to reading comprehension. For example, the phrase "over the mountain" is more easily read and understood in totem, as opposed to focusing on each word separately.

Math Strategies

In comparison to language arts handicaps, mathematical disabilities have been significantly less researched (Bender, 2008, p. 218). For mathematical word problems, current best practices emphasize on teaching students to focus on systematically organizing key facts. This ability to derive key math data from writing is crucial to word problem solving. Furthermore, mathematic stories should be based on familiar scenarios that students can easily understand and relate to (Browder, et al., 2012, p. 29). Students that have reading comprehension disabilities are faced with additional hardships with mathematical word problem solving and may require more intensive assistance (Bender, 2008, p. 222). To compensate, teachers can read aloud the story while students follow along in an effort to relieve the additional stress of reading comprehension and allow the student to focus on the mathematical aspect of the word problem (Browder, et al., 2012, p. 30).

Mathematical disabilities that do not involve additional reading comprehension difficulties are classified as nonverbal disabilities (Hallahan, Kauffman & Pullen, 2009, p. 201). Among the most accepted approaches to understanding math skill difficulties is the concept of number sense. Number sense refers to the difficulty, or lack of understanding of the core principles that makes mathematics work. For example, the concept of quantity of fewer versus greater and more or less than is imperative to solving all mathematical problems. Likewise, a student struggling with understanding place value, that is, that the order of numbers changes the numerical value, will have extreme difficulty in problem solving (Bender, 2008, p. 220). Thus, the most basic and rudimentary math skills require number sense (p.229). Number sense can be stressed through physical representation of numbers and manually added and subtracted. To illustrate, a student can be asked to group several pencils together, count them and write down the number. Then, additional pencils are added (or removed) from the group resulting in a new sum total. This exercise will concrete the number system from an abstract concept to a now physical and realistic representation via the pencils. Moreover, by counting to at least twenty one pencils, this activity can demonstrate the concept of place value, as the number one and two represent distinct numbers as twelve and twenty one respectively (pp. 229-230).

Chapter 14: Further best practices: Step by Step and Scaffolding

Due to the intricacies of special education, it behooves educators to be cognizant of proper instructional strategies. This chapter centers on step by step techniques and scaffolding. Moreover, each method is discussed individually, as a best practice for special education and compared and contrasted with each other.

Step By Step

Step by step techniques focus on providing small increments of data with associated tasks or assignments that allow students to be guided in a comfortable learning pace. Step by step best practices are appropriate for the entire spectrum of special education and comprise a variety of techniques (Rafferty, 2010, p. 51). To illustrate, Rafferty (pp. 51-52) notes that strategy instruction coupled with goal setting can be used provide a step by step practice in which the student has a clear and visible academic goal that is presented in a non-overwhelming fashion. This is especially important for students with special needs who often benefit when curricula requirements are clearly explained (Olson, Platt & Dieker, 2008, p.141).

Scaffolding

According to Lev Vygotsky, scaffolding is a guided learning theory that promotes self-efficacy in learning via adequate support from the teacher and curricula (Lamport, Graves, & Ward, 2012, p. 57). As such, the goal remains for the student to actively participate and apply previous information in new scenarios (Olson, Platt & Dieker, 2008, p.148). Lev Vygotsky maintains that learning is optimally achieved in the Zone of Proximal Development (ZPD) which is the area right in the middle between what the student is able to learn by his or herself and learning that requires direction from an educator (Raymond, 2012, p. 196). Raymond (pp.196-197) notes that it is essential for teachers of special education to be cognizant of potential academic challenges for their students vis-à-vis how the concept of ZPD pertains to exceptional students.

In particular, using scaffolding, the educator provides resources for the students to figure out the assignment on their own. As the student masters the content, scaffolding is slowly reduced with the ultimate goal of eliminating scaffolding in its entirety (Lamport, Graves, & Ward, 2012, p. 57).

Olson, Platt and Dieker (2008, p.149) provide a practical example of the scaffolding technique to employ for reading comprehension. If a student is struggling with pronouncing the full word, scaffolding would dictate that instead of the teacher repeating the word until the student can pronounce it, the teacher should confirm the correct part of the word and focus on the remaining part until the student can figure out the remainder. The feelings of self-efficacy and self-worth emanating from figuring it out can further bolster a students drive to continue in his or her educational goals in school. Nevertheless, it is prudent that educators be cognizant of the academic ability of the student lest scaffolding lesson cause undue stress and frustration which can ultimately result in the opposite results. Other useful scaffolding supports can include cues, prompts or even partial answers can be acceptable based on the teachers discretion (Raymond, 2008, p. 196).

Comparison and Contrast of Step By Step and Scaffolding

Albeit step by step and scaffolding are two distinct methodologies, there exists a certain amount of overlap. Perhaps the most obvious overlap is the concept of presenting information in an organized fashion to bolster student comprehension and mastery. However, whereas scaffolding promotes self-mastery and efficacy, step by step procedures focus on teacher delivery. One may surmise that best practices dictate the preference of one method based on the specific considerations of the collective student needs and classroom dynamics.

Another important similarity is the adaptability of both methods. Each method is mutually able to provide a customizable learning experience. This is especially important for the exceptional student population, as learning is often catered for the individual learner (Raymond, 2008, p. 197).

Chapter 15: Self-determination and IEP

A vital aspect of special education is to prepare exceptional students for achieve self-determination in adulthood. Self-determination is the ability to live independently and act according to one's personal preference with appropriate life skills (Hallahan, Kaufman & Pullen, 2009, pp. 171-172). This chapter will explore the concept of self-determination and advocacy of students with disabilities and document proven methods of transitional assessment to facilitate this goal.

Self-determination goals

Although it is difficult to predict if an exceptional student will have a successful transition to adulthood, Hallahan, et al. (2009, p. 216) note that research indicates that students who display an extraordinary degree of perseverance coupled with a realistic understanding of their shortcomings and a strong and positive social network of friends or family are most likely to succeed. Furthermore, Denney and Daviso (2012, p. 46) add that exceptional students that clearly think out their goals and can adapt to their environment are most often able to adjust to adulthood.

Transitional assessment for adult independence

A major component of special education is to provide the skills and tools necessary to reach self-determination through the students Individualized Education Program (IEP) (Hallahan, et al., 2009, p. 171). To facilitate the creation of a proper IEP, transitional and vocational assessment tools are used to evaluate a student's strengths and weaknesses. It is common for transitional and vocational assessment to viewed in three distinct stages. Initial assessment, generally prior to age fourteen, consists of an ingathering of all previous data relating to general special education. Further assessment, in particular to cultivating goals for future vocation is then introduced. This is followed with the final stage which consists of assessment concentrating on real vocational results (Taylor, 2009, p. 378).

In recording the various vocational assessment tools and methods, Taylor (pp. 377-378) notes that although formerly only formal assessment tools were used for vocational assessment, it has become accepted to employ informal methods as well. An important method of informal assessment is interviewing the exceptional student. A popular and practical example of this evaluation is the Brigance Life Skills Inventory test which can garner a large corpus of information of a student's personality, habits and work style in best providing the student with practical recommendations of future vocation (Taylor, 2009, pp. 383-384; Brigance, 1995, p. 313). The Brigance Life Skills Inventory test provides an aptitude rating scale of a rating of one (never observed) to five (always observed) in areas relating to the student's ability to work with others, appropriate ability to complete assigned tasks, ask questions if needed and general knowledge of proper work ethics (Brigance, 1995, p. 313). Moreover, the Brigance Life Skills Inventory takes into account the exceptional student's self-advocacy and self-determination by involving the student by inquiring of their interests pertaining to future vocation. For example, questions regarding a student's preference to working solo versus working in a group are discussed, as well as questions regarding location of job. Hence, questions posed include: Does the student enjoy working outside, or prefer a desk job? Does the student need to work close to home or he she can commute to work?

Self-advocacy and the IEP process

Regardless of the method of transitional assessment employed, the active participation of the student in preparation of the IEP and prevocational training is of vital importance (Denney & Daviso, 2012, p.48). Unfortunately, research indicates that although sixty-eight percent of teachers said they explained the IEP process to their students, only forty-four percent of students advanced their own goals during the IEP meeting, with a mere five percent prepared or led the meeting (Denney & Daviso, 2012, p. 47). Indeed, Denney and Daviso (*supra*) note that only eight percent of teachers and school personnel reported being satisfied with current levels of student participation. Thus, it is evident that practical devices to promote exceptional student's self-advocacy be promoted and included in curricula. Denney and Daviso (pp. 48-49) posit that teachers should stimulate students with disabilities to take an active role in establishing short and long term personal and educational goals. Therefore, when a student is accustomed to being involved in decisions, he or she will be more likely to self-advocate and participate in IEP meetings, and ultimately, successful transition skills. Additionally, teachers must remember to maintain high expectations for all students regardless of disabilities. Stress must be placed on an individual student's positive qualities and abilities. Thus, students will focus on their strengths and will feel empowered to be assertive and bolster their positive self-image.

Chapter 16: Parent-School relationships: IEP in focus

Parent-teacher interactions play a vital role in providing a full educational experience. This chapter explores the relationships between parents of exceptional students and school personnel. Different reactions to these interactions noted in ethnic and or social groups are noted, especially in terms of methods employed by parents requesting special education services and in preparation of the Individualized Education Program (IEP.) Additionally, legal requirements of teachers in providing parental interactions are discussed.

The role of parents

A team approach between home and school is optimal for overall student educational impact and growth (Jones & Gansle, 2010, p.23). Different parents react differently upon finding out their child has a disability. Research conducted by Trainor (2010, pp. 252-253) has shown that Caucasian parents (regardless of socioeconomic grouping) described a feeling of relief upon ascertaining the nature their child's diagnosis. These parents felt empowered by finding out the name of the disability so that they focused on remediation for the child's needs. This parent body used their newfound information to seek professional advice outside of school (Trainor, 2010, p. 252). In contrast, African American parents expressed uncertainty and agitation; for concern that labeling their child as exceptional implied limitations resulting in both teacher and student low expectation for success (Trainor, 2010, p. 252). Trainer (2010, p. 257) posits these differences in approach to knowledge of dominant culture delivery and command of language. Those who were already familiar with the dominant culture's parlance were viewed as having a certain adroitness in negotiating the special education services they needed for their children. Additionally, Trainor (2010, p. 260) notes that Caucasian parents viewed classroom inclusion favorably and advocated inclusion for their exceptional student children. However, African American parents did not view inclusion as a priority. Trainor (2010, pp. 246-247) further postulates that educators are not above critique of the aforementioned data, for teachers themselves play an active role in communicating with parents. Many Caucasian teachers are not sufficiently aware of the social background of parents various ethnicities, and the proper communicative methods to employ when meeting such parents.

Contrary to research data collected by Trainor, Jones and Gansle (2010, p. 24) report a contrast of perception of labeling not in terms of ethnic grouping, but rather, based on socioeconomic status or lower education of the parent body. Parents from lower socioeconomic and with lower levels of education were reported as having less concerned and interested in participation with school personnel than parents with high socioeconomic status or higher education.

Legalities and the role of teachers

The Individuals with Disabilities Education Act (IDEA) mandates that school personnel provide parents of exceptional students with a method of home-school collaboration (Trainor, 2010, p. 245). An important point of interaction is the meeting in determining an exceptional student's IEP (Hallahan, Kauffman & Pullen, 2009, pp. 20, 29). IDEA requires a parent (or legal guardian) to be consulted during the IEP meeting in preparing the IEP. Additionally, IDEA requires school personnel to inform parents in advance of the date of the IEP meeting, as well as the ability to agree to that date (Fish, 2008, p. 8). As discussed in the preceding paragraph, not all parents react in a uniform manner to this meeting. However, practically all family theorists concur that parents and school personnel that work in unison is key to the success of an IEP (Hallahan, et al., 2009, p. 133). Fish (2008, p. 10) conducted research to ascertain parent's feelings about the IEP meeting and experience. Fish records that 63 percent of interviewed parents felt positive about the IEP experience, as opposed to 16 percent who disagreed. Additionally, 47 percent of parents reported that the topic of student objectives and goals was discussed sufficiently in the meeting. In terms of disagreements with school personnel, 20 percent found student placement to be the main controversy, and 18 percent reported issues regarding services to be their primary disagreement (Fish, 2008, p.10).

Parental knowledge of special education and IEP

Not all parents know enough about IEP. Fish (2008, p.11) notes that 24 percent of parents felt their school did not convey sufficient information and guidance of the IEP process, and an additional 10 percent felt that way strongly. In contrast, only 32 percent of parents were satisfied in the knowledge school personnel conveyed regarding the IEP process, with only an additional 16 percent who agreed strongly. This data behooves educators to be mindful of parent's knowledge, or lack of, of the IEP process when initiating IEP meetings and discussions. Fish (2008, p.11) opines that schools should provide especial training in proper IEP meeting preparation to those educators that will be conducting and or attending IEP meetings with parents. Additionally, teachers must be mindful not to inundate parents with too much information at once, and use technical educational terms in moderation (Hallahan, Kauffman & Pullen, 2009, p. 127; Fish, 2008, p. 13; Trainor, 2010, p. 24). Although educators should not use too much educational jargon to the parent body, Fish's (2008) research indicates that educators must use clear, concise language to parents and cannot assume parents already know the basics of IEP. A popular school method is to dispense literature on the rudimentary principles and methodology of the IEP system and to make this available to parents of exceptional students prior to the IEP meeting. However, Hallahan, et al. (2009, p. 129) suggest that some linguistically and or culturally different families may be more comfortable in obtaining information in family support groups. Overall, the majority of parents interviewed stated that their involvement enhanced the IEP meeting, and that their input had a practical influence on the creation of the IEP (Fish, 2008, p.12).

It is prudent that teachers be cognizant that education is but one factor of a child's development and some parents will regulate curricula and other aspects of the IEP to the discretion of the school (Hallahan, et al., 2009, pp. 130-131). Data collected by Trainor (2010, p. 24) suggests that the majority of parents with a lower level of involvement of the IEP process are from low socioeconomic backgrounds or lower levels of education. Nevertheless, this should not be viewed as necessarily negligent, as lack of participation may be due to schedule conflicts or other family responsibilities (Hallahan, et al., 2009, p. 131; Trainor, 2010, p.25).

Additional methods of parent-teacher discourse

Albeit the IEP meeting plays a pivotal role in parent-teacher discourse, this relationship is by no means limited to the IEP meeting. Additional practical methods to facilitate positive parental interactions involve the use of sending home notes. The home-note (otherwise known as the home-contingency) program involves updating the parents via a note sent home that can inform parents on a variety of things (Hallahan, Kauffman & Pullen, 2009, p 135). For example, a note can notify parents of homework assignments, refer to behavioral issues, or consist of annotations. The ultimate goal of the home-note program is to provide current updates on a student's progress, or lack thereof, and allow parents to reinforce performance of concepts taught in school (Hallahan, et al., 2009, pp. 135-136). This writer speculates that as access to internet service is becoming even more widespread, the physical home-note system will eventually be replaced by e-mail notes. This has the additional advantage that the teacher does not need to wait to the next morning to view correspondence with a parent, but can already be aware of parental reaction to the message as soon as e-mail is checked. Thus, a teacher can be better prepared to manage a potential issue for the next day.

Another important aspect of parental involvement is parent-teacher conferences (Hallahan, et al., 2009, p. 134). Parent-teacher conferences provide an opportunity for the educator to learn more about the student's background, and an opportunity for the educator to discuss various issues with the parent (Hallahan, et al., 2009, p. 134).

References

Bender, W. N. (2008). *Learning disabilities: Characteristics, identification, and teaching strategies* (6th ed.). Boston, MA: Pearson/Allyn and Bacon.

Berkeley, S., Mastropieri, M. A., & Scruggs, T. E. (2011). Reading comprehension strategy instruction and attribution retraining for secondary students with learning and other mild disabilities. *Journal of Learning Disabilities, 44*(18), 18-33. doi:10.1177/0022219410371677

Brigance, A. H. (1995). Brigance diagnostic life skills inventory. *Intervention In School & Clinic, 30*(5), 313.

Brookhart, S. M. (2011). Educational assessment knowledge and skills for teachers. *Educational Assessment Knowledge and Skills for Teachers, 30*(1), 3-12. doi:10.1111/j.1745-3992.2010.00195.x

Browder, D. M., Trela, K., Courtade, G. R., Jimenez, B. A., Knight, V., & Flowers, C. (2012). Teaching mathematics and science standards to students with moderate and severe developmental disabilities. *Journal Of Special Education, 46*(1), 26-35. doi:10.1177/0022466910369942

Denney, S. C., & Daviso, A. W. (2012). Self-Determination: A critical component of education. *American Secondary Education, 40*(2), 43-51.

Drahota, A., Sterling, L., Hwang, W., & Wood, J. J. (2013). Daily living skills in school-age children with and without anxiety disorders. *British Journal of Clinical Psychology, 52*(1), 107-112. doi:10.1111/bjc.12015

Fish, W. W. (2008). The IEP meeting: Perceptions of parents of students who receive special education services. *Preventing School Failure, 53*(1), 8-14.

Geng, G. (2011). Investigation of teachers' verbal and non-verbal strategies for managing attention deficit hyperactivity disorder (ADHD) students' behaviours within a classroom environment. *Australian Journal of Teacher Education, 36*(7), 17-30.

Haager, D., & Vaughn, S. (1995). Parent, teacher, peer, and self-reports of the social competence of students with learning disabilities. *Journal Of Learning Disabilities, 28*(4), 205-215.

Hallahan, D. P., Kauffman, J. M., & Pullen, P. C. (2009). *Exceptional learners: An introduction to special education* (11th ed.). Boston, MA: Pearson/Allyn & Bacon.

Hay, I., Elias, G., Fielding-Barnsley, R., Homel, R., & Freiberg, K. (2007). Language Delays, Reading Delays, and Learning Difficulties: Interactive Elements Requiring Multidimensional Programming. *Journal of Learning Disabilities, 40*(5), 400-409. doi:10.1177/00222194070400050301

Idan, O., & Margalit, M. (2012). Socioemotional self-perceptions, family climate, and hopeful thinking among students with learning disabilities and typically achieving students from the same classes. *Journal of Learning Disabilities, 20*(10), 1-18. doi:10.1177/0022219412439608

Imeraj, L., Antrop, I., Sonuga-Barke, E., Deboutte, D., Deschepper, E., Bal, S., & Roeyers, H. (2013). The impact of instructional context on classroom on-task behavior: A matched comparison of children with ADHD and non-ADHD classmates. *Journal of School Psychology, 51*(4), 487–498.

Jones, B. A., & Gansle, K. A. (2010). The effects of a mini-conference, socioeconomic status, and parent education on perceived and actual parent participation in individual education program meetings. *Research In The Schools, 17*(2), 23-38.

Lamport, M. A., Graves, L., & Ward, A. (2012). Special needs students in inclusive classrooms: The impact of social interaction on educational outcomes for learners with emotional and behavioral disabilities. *European Journal of Business and Social Sciences, 1*(5), 54-69.

Luke, S. D., & Schwartz, A. (2007). Assessment and accommodations. *Evidence for Education, 2*(1), 1-10.

Martinussen, R., & Major, A. (2011). Working memory weaknesses in students with ADHD: Implications for instruction. *Theory Into Practice, 50*(1), 68-75.

Special Education: Best Practices in Focus

Mayer, M., Lochman, J., & Van Acker, R. (2005). Introduction to the special issue: Cognitive-behavioral interventions with students With EBD. *Behavioral Disorders, 30*(3), 197–212.

Olson, J. L., Platt, J. M., & Dieker, L. (2008). *Teaching children and adolescents with special needs* (5th ed.). Upper Saddle River, N.J: Pearson Education.

Ornstein, A. C., & Hunkins, F. P. (2009). *Curriculum: Foundations, principles, and issues* (5th ed.). Boston, MA: Pearson.

Pang, K. (2010). Creating stimulating learning and thinking using new models of activity-based learning and metacognitive-based activities. *Journal of College Teaching & Learning, 7*(4), 29-38.

Pfiffner, L. J., Villodas, M., Kaiser, N., Rooney, M., & McBurnett, K. (2013). Educational outcomes of a collaborative school–home behavioral intervention for ADHD. *School Psychology Quarterly, 28*(1), 25–36. doi:10.1037/spq0000016

Phillipo, K. (2010). Teachers providing social and emotional support: A study of advisor role enactment in small high schools. *Teachers College Record, 112*(8), 2258-2293.

Psychology: Epigenetics. (2013). In *Encyclopaedia Britannica*. Retrieved from http://www.britannica.com.proxy1.ncu.edu/EBchecked/topic/481700/psychology/288098/Epigenetics

Rafferty, L. A. (2010). Step-by-step: Teaching students to self-monitor. *Teaching Exceptional Children, 43*(2), 50-58.

Raymond, E. B. (2012). *Learners with mild disabilities: A characteristics approach* (4th ed.). Boston, MA: Pearson.

Robinson, T. (2007). Cognitive behavioral interventions: Strategies to help students make wise behavioral choices. *Beyond Behavior, 17*(1), 7-13.

Robinson, T. R., Smith, S. W., & Miller, M. D. (2002). Effect of cognitive behavioral intervention on responses to anger by middle school students with chronic behavior problems. *Behavioral Disorders, 27*(3), 256-271.

Settipani, C. A., & Kendall, P. C. (2013). Social functioning in youth with anxiety disorders: Association with anxiety severity and outcomes from cognitive-behavioral therapy. *Child Psychiatry & Human Development, 44*(1), 1-18. doi:10.1007/s10578-012-0307-0

Stenhoff, D. M., & Lignugaris, B. (2007). A review of the effects of peer tutoring on students with mild disabilities in secondary settings. *Exceptional Children, 74*(1), 8-30.

Taylor, R. L. (2009). *Assessment of exceptional students: Educational and psychological procedures* (8th ed.). Upper Saddle River, NJ: Pearson/Merrill.

Thomas, P. G., & Kevin, S. S. (2010). The relation between emotional and behavioral disorders and school-based violence. *Aggression And Violent Behavior, 15*, 349–356. doi:10.1016/j.avb.2010.06.003

Trainor, A. A. (2010). Reexamining the promise of parent participation in special education: An analysis of cultural and social capital. *Anthropology & Education Quarterly, 41*(3), 245-263. doi:10.1111/j.1548-1492.2010.01086.x.

Vaughn, S., Elbaum, B., Schumm, J., & Hughes, M. (1998). Social outcomes for students with and without learning disabilities in inclusive classrooms. *Journal Of Learning Disabilities, 31*(5), 428-436.

Webber, J., & Plotts, C. A. (2008). *Emotional and behavioral disorders: Theory and practice* (5th ed.). Boston, MA: Pearson/Allyn and Bacon.

Wiener, J., & Tardif, C. Y. (2004). Social and emotional functioning of children with learning disabilities: Does special education placement make a difference? *Learning Disabilities Research & Practice, 19*(1), 20-32.

Williams, J. A. (2010). Taking on the role of Questioner: Revisiting reciprocal teaching. *Reading Teacher, 64*(4), 278-281. doi: 10.1598/RT.64.4.6

Wood, F. H. (1995). Emotional/behavioral disorders and the `Ziegarnik effect'. *Education & Treatment Of Children (ETC), 18*(3), 216-220.

Zirpoli, T. J. (2008). *Behavior management: Applications for teachers* (5th ed.). Upper Saddle River, NJ: Pearson/Merrill Prentice Hall.

Special Education: Best Practices in Focus

Made in the USA
San Bernardino, CA
30 July 2016